The Forward Book
of Poetry 1999

FORWARD PUBLISHING
LONDON

First published in Great Britain by
Forward Publishing · 84-86 Regent Street · London W1R 6DD
in association with
Faber and Faber · 3 Queen Square · London WC1N 3AU

ISBN 0 571 196381 (paperback)

Compilation copyright © Forward Publishing 1998
For copyright on individual poems see acknowledgements page 9
Foreword copyright © Geordie Greig 1998
Front cover illustration by Kevin O'Brien

Reprographics by Colourpath
Soho · London

Printed by Redwood Books Ltd.
Kennet Way · Trowbridge · Wilts. BA14 8RN

To Barnaby Rogerson

Preface

WELCOME TO THE SEVENTH FORWARD BOOK OF POETRY, the result of
the deliberations of this year's judges of the Forward Poetry Prizes.
As always, their selection gives a fascinating picture of contemporary
poetry and contemporary life. For poetry lovers and new initiates, the
Forward Book of Poetry will, I hope, be as intriguing and as colourful an
anthology as its predecessors.

In creating the *Forward Book of Poetry* and its partner in verse,
National Poetry Day, we at the Forward Poetry Trust have received
help and finance from a number of sources. We would like to thank
Gordon Kerr at Waterstone's, Jeffery Tolman and Peter Cunard at
Tolman Cunard, and Lex Fenwick at Bloomberg for financial and
personal support.

We would also like to thank the many poetry commandos who help
to make our poetry festivities complete: our judges for this year's
prize (Geordie Greig, Josephine Hart, Simon Armitage, Jamie
McKendrick and Allison Pearson), our partners at the BBC,
The Poetry Society, Colman Getty, Faber and Faber and everyone at
Forward Publishing. This year we also received generous help from
the National Year of Reading, the Department of Culture, Media and
Sport and Simon Elvin.

Thank you all, and happy reading.

William Sieghart

Foreword

FORTY YEARS AGO, T. S. ELIOT warned that a nation which ceases to produce poetry will in the long run cease to be able to enjoy and even understand the great poetry of its own past. More recently, in a lecture at Oxford, Seamus Heaney sounded another powerful wake-up call: "Poetry cannot afford to lose its fundamentally self-delighting inventiveness, its joy in being a process of language as well as a representative of things in the world."

Well, the good news is that poetry has never been so healthy in terms of sheer volume published. This year saw a new record created with the sales of one particular book of verse: Ted Hughes's *Birthday Letters*, which for several weeks was number one in *The Sunday Times* bestseller list. The bad news is that this was a rare, isolated example of poetry's popularity. On the whole the rise in the amount of poetry published has not brought about an increase in the number of people who read it. It is still a minority interest, which is why this anthology, published on National Poetry Day, is proudly proselytising; it is designed to alert as many people as possible to the joy of, challenge of, and the need for poetry. *The Forward Book of Poetry 1999* is an appealing introduction to the best contemporary poetry.

The process of selection for this anthology was not easy. For more than five weeks, a seemingly never-ending supply of poetry books popped through the front door, at alarmingly frequent intervals, and in surprisingly bulky packages, as I and the other four judges set about trying to select just 50 poems from a total of more than 8,000 which had been submitted. As we ploughed through the daunting pile of 230 volumes and an additional sheaf of individual poems published in magazines and newspapers, our dilemma was what to choose. Samuel Johnson's irritatingly unhelpful thoughts on the definition of poetry kept springing to mind as we wrestled with our choices.

Boswell: "Sir, what is poetry?"

Johnson: "Why sir, it is much easier to say what it is not. We all know what light is: but it is not easy to tell what it is."

Each of the judges, the poets Simon Armitage and Jamie McKendrick, the novelist Josephine Hart, the newspaper columnist Allison Pearson, and myself, the Literary Editor of *The Sunday Times* brought our own divergent views on what makes a good poem during a lively five hour meeting, when we also decided on a shortlist for the categories of Best Collection, Best First Collection and Best Individual Poem Published. At the time this book had to go to press our judging process was still incomplete. We had not yet chosen the overall winners from our shortlists, but were pleasantly surprised by how much more we agreed than disagreed on the shortlist after impassioned, forthright debate.

We all felt that a good anthology is only useful if it is born out of a desire to discover and is created in a spirit of excitement and generosity. Sir Walter Raleigh said that an anthology should be like having all the plums and orange peel picked out of a cake. We found many plums and much orange peel from which to choose, but there was also a lot of material which was easily discarded.

Reading 8,000 poems, one after another, is not the recommended way to enjoy poetry. Our mass sampling was a roller coaster ride with a mesmerising view of every possible facet of life at the cusp of the millennium: a father's agony over his daughter's anorexia, the mass suicide at Jonestown, blokish feminism, the pain and gain of passion, deportation, deprivation, space exploration, even Zen in the Outer Hebrides. It seemed, at times, as if the whole of the natural world had come before us as wasps, whales, elks, owls, poppies, lupins, mistletoe, shrimps and fossil unicorns crowded into view. The wider world came to us as we read poems by writers born in Malawi, Jamaica, Texas, Iran, Sierra Leone, Canada, Australia, and, of course, all over Britain and Ireland. The competition was truly open, with poet-parsons, space explorers, ramblers, jazzy urban guerrillas, gay activists, teachers, political dissidents as well as ordinary people bringing extraordinary epiphanies from their lives.

The Forward Poetry Prize is now an important event in the literary calendar. It singles out new and tested talents. It was with a sense of humility and difficulty that we judges made our final choices, aware that in the best of all possible worlds we would have liked more time to read and re-read some poems.

We would like to thank William Sieghart of Forward Publishing for his vision and generosity in establishing the Forward prizes and making sure they prosper along with the annual anthology. We are also indebted to Margot Weale of Colman Getty who was a charming, calming and diplomatic administrator of the competition.

As the process of judging will not be complete before the publication of this book, the prize winners will not be known until after this anthology is in the bookshops. We recommend that you buy all the shortlisted volumes, and see if your choice tallies with ours. Whatever happens, you are guaranteed many hours of pleasure.

Geordie Greig

Acknowledgements

Peter Armstrong · NORTH OF THUNDER BAY OR HIGHWAY 61 RECONSTITUTED ·
    Poetry Review

Kate Bingham · ETUDES · *Cohabitation* · seren

Olivia Byard · WHORES IN AMSTERDAM · *From a Benediction* · Peterloo Poets

Olivia Byard · THEFT · *From a Benediction* · Peterloo Poets

Anne Carson · GOD'S JUSTICE · *Glass and God* · Cape Poetry

Anne Carson · FROM THE FALL OF ROME: A TRAVELLER'S GUIDE, LXIV ·
    Glass and God · Cape Poetry

David Constantine · THE WASPS · *The Pelt of Wasps* · Bloodaxe Books

Sarah Corbett · WOOD SISTER · *the red wardrobe* · seren

Sarah Corbett · THE RED WARDROBE · *the red wardrobe* · seren

Fred D'Aguiar · FROM BILL OF RIGHTS (P.27)· *Bill of Rights* · Chatto & Windus

Mark Doty · GOLDEN RETRIEVALS · *Sweet Machine* · Cape Poetry

Greg Delanty · THE COMPOSITOR · *The Hellbox* · Oxford University Press

Ian Duhig · JUNGLE · *Nominies* · Bloodaxe Books

Antony Dunn · THE KISS · *Pilots and Navigators* · Oxford University Press

Douglas Dunn · A EUROPEAN DREAM · Times Literary Supplement

Colin Falck · 26 · *Post-modern Love* · Stride

Paul Farley · TREACLE · *The Boy from the Chemist is Here to See You* · Picador

Paul Farley · LAWS OF GRAVITY · *The Boy from the Chemist is Here to See You* ·
    Picador

Lavinia Greenlaw · READING AKHMATOVA IN MIDWINTER ·
    A World Where News Travelled Slowly · Faber and Faber

Philip Gross · FROM THE WASTING GAME, 12 · *The Wasting Game* ·
    Bloodaxe Books

Sophie Hannah · OVER AND ELM AND I · Poetry Review

David Harsent · THE CURATOR · *A Bird's Idea of Flight* · Faber and Faber

Geoff Hattersley · 'ON THE BUSES' WITH DOSTOYEVSKY ·
    'On the Buses' with Dostoyevsky · Bloodaxe Books

Ted Hughes · FLOUNDERS · *Birthday Letters* · Faber and Faber

Ted Hughes · YOUR PARIS · *Birthday Letters* · Faber and Faber

Peter Joliffe · LACUNA · The Sunday Times

Gwyneth Lewis · ANCIENT AUNTIES · *Zero Gravity* · Bloodaxe Books

Gwyneth Lewis · FROM ZERO GRAVITY, VI · *Zero Gravity* · Bloodaxe Books

Thomas Lynch · THE RIDDANCE · *Still Life in Milford* · Cape Poetry

Derek Mahon · LANDSCAPE (AFTER BAUDELAIRE) · *The Yellow Book* · Gallery Books

Derek Mahon · DEATH IN BANGOR · *The Yellow Book* · Gallery Books

Jack Mapanje · SKIPPING WITHOUT ROPE · *Skipping without Ropes* ·
    Bloodaxe Books

Glyn Maxwell · MY GRANDFATHER AT THE POOL · *The Breakage* · Faber and Faber

Glyn Maxwell · DEEP SORRINESS ATONEMENT SONG · *The Breakage* ·
    Faber and Faber

Paul Muldoon · AFTERMATH · The Sunday Times

Conor O'Callaghan · THE SWIMMING POOL · The Sunday Times

Marita Over · THE DAFFODILS · *Other Lilies* · The Frogmore Press

Ruth Padel · ICICLES ROUND A TREE IN DUMFRIESSHIRE ·
    Rembrandt Would Have Loved You · Chatto & Windus

Peter Porter · BASTA SANGUE · Times Literary Supplement

Sheenagh Pugh · ENVYING OWEN BEATTIE · New Welsh Review

Lesley Saunders · THE USES OF GREEK · The Rialto

Joan Jobe Smith · THE POW WOW CAFÉ · *The Pow Wow Café* ·
    Smith/Doorstep Books

Jean Sprackland · THE RINGLET · *Tattoos for Mothers Day* · Spike

Jean Sprackland · IN THE PLANETARIUM · *Tattoos for Mothers Day* · Spike

Martin Stannard · SEEING HAPPY · Poetry Quarterly Review

Paul Summers · THE LAST BUS · *The Last Bus* · Iron Press

Matthew Sweeney · GOODBYE TO THE SKY · *The Bridal Suite* · Cape Poetry

Chris Wallace-Crabbe · YEARS ON · *Whirling* · Oxford University Press

David Wheatley · LYING IN LATE · *Thirst* · Gallery Books

David Wheatley · BRAY HEAD · *Thirst* · Gallery Books

Andrew Wilson · VODAFONE · *Des for Pres* · Smith/Doorstep Books

Contents

The Best Collection Poems

Anne Carson

GOD'S JUSTICE

In the beginning there were days set aside for various tasks.
On the day He was to create justice
God got involved in making a dragonfly

and lost track of time.
It was about two inches long
with turquoise dots all down its back like Lauren Bacall.

God watched it bend its tiny wire elbows
as it set about cleaning the transparent case of its head.
The eye globes mounted on the case

rotated this way and that
as it polished every angle.
Inside the case

which was glassy black like the windows of a downtown bank
God could see the machinery humming
and He watched the hum

travel all the way down turquoise dots to the end of the tail
and breathe off as light.
Its black wings vibrated in and out.

LXIV

There are three ways to master death.
Here is the third one (the one
Anna Xenia told me

on the way home from Orvieto).
Signorelli is painting late in his studio
when they carry in his son,

killed in a riot.
He sits up all night with the body,
making sketch after sketch

and throwing them into a pile.
From that time
all his angels

have the one
same
face.

Ted Hughes

Was that a happy day? From Chatham
Down at the South end of the Cape, our map
Somebody's optimistic assurance,
We set out to row. We got ourselves
Into mid-channel. The tide was flowing. We hung
Anchored. Northward-pulling, our baited leads
Bounced and bounced the bottom. For three hours –
Two or three sea-robins. Cruisers
Folded us under their bow-waves, we bobbed up,
Happy enough. But the wind
Smartened against us, and the tide turned, roughening,
Dragged seaward. We rowed. We rowed. We
Saw we weren't going to make it. We turned,
Cutting downwind for the sand-bar, beached
And wondered what next. It was there
I found a horse-shoe crab's carapace, perfect,
No bigger than a bee, in honey-pale cellophane.
No way back. But big, good America found us.
A power-boat and a pilot of no problems.
He roped our boat to his stern and with all his family
Slammed back across the channel into the wind,
The spray scything upwards, our boat behind
Twisting across the wake-boil – a hectic
Four or five minutes and he cast us off
In the lee of the land, but a mile or more
From our dock. We toiled along inshore. We came
To a back-channel, under beach-house gardens – marsh grass,
Wild, original greenery of America,
Mud-slicks and fiddler-crab warrens, as we groped
Towards the harbour. Gloom-rich water. Something
Suggested easy plenty. We lowered baits,
And out of about six feet of water
Six or seven feet from land, we pulled up flounders

Big as big plates, till all our bait had gone.
After our wind-burned, head-glitter day of emptiness,
And the slogging row for our lives, and the rescue,
Suddenly out of water easy as oil
The sea piled our boat with its surplus. And the day
Curled out of brilliant, arduous morning,
Through wind-hammered perilous afternoon,
Salt-scoured, to a storm-gold evening, a luxury
Of rowing among the dream-yachts of the rich
Lolling at anchor off the play-world pier.

How tiny an adventure
To stay so monumental in our marriage,
A slight ordeal of all that might be,
And a small thrill-breath of what many live by,
And a small prize, a toy miniature
Of the life that might have bonded us
Into a single animal, a single soul –

It was a visit from the goddess, the beauty
Who was poetry's sister – she had come
To tell poetry she was spoiling us.
Poetry listened, maybe, but we heard nothing
And poetry did not tell us. And we
Only did what poetry told us to do.

Your Paris, I thought, was American.
I wanted to humour you.
When you stepped, in a shatter of exclamations,
Out of the Hôtel des Deux Continents
Through frame after frame,
Street after street, of Impressionist paintings,
Under the chestnut shades of Hemingway,
Fitzgerald, Henry Miller, Gertrude Stein,
I kept my Paris from you. My Paris
Was only just not German. The capital
Of the Occupation and old nightmare.
I read each bullet scar in the Quai stonework
With an eerie familiar feeling,
And stared at the stricken, sunny exposure of pavement
Beneath it. I had rehearsed
Carefully, over and over, just those moments –
Most of my life, it seemed. While you
Called me Aristide Bruant and wanted
To draw *les toits*, and your ecstasies ricocheted
Off the walls patched and scabbed with posters –
I heard the contrabasso counterpoint
In my dog-nosed pondering analysis
Of café chairs where the SS mannequins
Had performed their *tableaux vivants*
So recently the coffee was still bitter
As acorns, and the waiters' eyes
Clogged with dregs of betrayal, reprisal, hatred.
I was not much ravished by the view of the roofs.
My Paris was a post-war utility survivor,
The stink of fear still hanging in the wardrobes,
Collaborateurs barely out of their twenties,
Every other face closed by the Camps
Or the Maquis. I was a ghostwatcher.
My perspectives were veiled by what rose
Like methane from the reopened

Mass grave of Verdun. For you all that
Was the anecdotal aesthetic touch
On Picasso's portrait
Of Apollinaire, with its proleptic
Marker for the bullet. And wherever
Your eye lit, your immaculate palette,
The thesaurus of your cries,
Touched in its tints and textures. Your lingo
Always like an emergency burn-off
To protect you from spontaneous combustion
Protected you
And your Paris. It was diesel aflame
To the dog in me. It scorched up
Every scent and sensor. And it sealed
The underground, your hide-out,
That chamber, where you still hung waiting
For your torturer
To remember his amusement. Those walls,
Raggy with posters, were your own flayed skin –
Stretched on your stone god.
What walked beside me was flayed,
One walking wound that the air
Coming against kept in a fever, wincing
To agonies. Your practised lips
Translated the spasms to what you excused
As your gushy burblings – which I decoded
Into a language, utterly new to me
With conjectural, hopelessly wrong meanings –
You gave me no hint how, at every corner,
My fingers linked in yours, you expected
The final face-to-face revelation
To grab your whole body. Your Paris
Was a desk in a *pension*
Where your letters
Waited for him unopened. Was a labyrinth
Where you still hurtled, scattering tears.
Was a dream where you could not

Wake or find the exit or
The Minotaur to put a blessed end
To the torment. What searching miles
Did you drag your pain
That were for me plain paving, albeit
Pecked by the odd, stray, historic bullet.
The mere dog in me, happy to protect you
From your agitation and your stone hours,
Like a guide dog, loyal to correct your stumblings,
Yawned and dozed and watched you calm yourself
With your anaesthetic – your drawing, as by touch,
Roofs, a traffic bollard, a bottle, me.

Gwyneth Lewis

ANCIENT AUNTIES

When Gladys put her handbag down
smack in the middle of standing stones
the dancing started. One by one

she touched the boulders, moved like a moon
from granite to sarsen, pacing out praise
for these prominent erections of man,

gliding past the North Pole of her bag
which smelt of lipstick and lavender.
Her pearls became bright satellites of her,

as she moved in ellipses, calling the gods
of darkness and chaos with parabolas
of wonder. No one can say we've gone to the dogs

while modern aunties are still in tune
with ancient eclipses, can stand alone
completing whole families of motionless stone.

VI

Last suppers, I fancy, are always wide-screen.
I see this one in snapshot: your brothers are rhymes
with you and each other. John has a shiner
from surfing. Already we've started counting time
backwards to zero. The Shuttle processed
out like an idol to its pagan pad.
It stands by its scaffold, being tended and blessed
by priestly technicians. You refuse to feel sad,
can't wait for your coming wedding with speed
out into weightlessness. We watch you dress
in your orange space suit, a Hindu bride,
with wires like henna for your loveliness.
You carry your helmet like a severed head.
We think of you as already dead.

Derek Mahon

LANDSCAPE

(after Baudelaire)

Chastely to write these eclogues I need to lie,
like the astrologers, in an attic next the sky
where, high among church spires, I can dream and hear
their grave hymns wind-blown to my ivory tower.
Chin in hand, up here in my apartment block,
I can see workshops full of noise and talk,
cranes and masts of the ocean-going city,
vast cloud formations dreaming about eternity.
I watch a foggy star glitter and shine
in the azure sky, a lamp at a window-pane,
smoke rising into the firmament like incense,
the moon dispensing its mysterious influence.
I watch for spring and summer, autumn too;
and when the winter comes, with silent snow,
I shut the shutters and close the curtains tight
to build my faerie palaces in the night
and dream of love and gardens, blue resorts,
white fountains weeping into marble courts,
birds chirping day and night, whatever notion
exites the infantile imagination...
Rattling the window with its riotous squabble
no mob distracts me from my writing-table;
for here I am, up to my usual tricks –
evoking spring-time on the least pretext,
extracting sunlight as my whims require,
my thoughts blazing for want of a real fire.

We stand – not many of us – in a new cemetery
on a cold hillside in the north of Co. Down
staring at an open grave or out to sea,
the lough half-hidden by great drifts of rain.
Only a few months since you were snug at home
in a bungalow glow, keeping provincial time
in the chimney corner, *News-Letter* and *Woman's Own*
on your knee, wool-gathering by Plato's firelight,
a grudging flicker of flame on anthracite.
Inactive since your husband died, your chief
concern the 'appearances' that ruled your life
in a neighbourhood of bay windows and stiff
gardens shivering in the salt sea air,
the rising-sun motif on door and gate,
you knew the secret history of needlework,
bread-bin and laundry basket awash with light,
the straight-backed chairs, the madly chiming clock.
The figure in the *Republic* returns to the cave,
a Dutch interior where cloud-shadows move,
to examine the intimate spaces, chest and drawer,
the lavender in the linen, the savings book,
the kitchen table silent with nobody there.
Shall we say the patience of an angel? No,
not unless angels be thought anxious too
and God knows you had reason to be; for yours
was an anxious time of nylon and bakelite,
market-driven hysteria on every fretwork radio,
your frantic kitsch decor designed for you
by thick industrialists and twisted ministers
('Nature's a bad example to simple folk'); and yet
with your wise monkeys and euphemistic 'Dresden' figurines,
your junk chinoiserie and coy pastoral scenes,
you too were a kind of artist, a rage-for-order freak
setting against a man's aesthetic of cars and golf
your ornaments and other breakable stuff.

Visible from your window the sixth-century
abbey church of Colum and Malachi,
'light of the world' once in the monastic ages,
home of antiphonary and the radiant pages
of shining scripture; though you had your own
idea of the beautiful, not unrelated to Tolstoy
but formed in a tough city of ships and linen,
Harland & Wolff, Mackie's, Gallaher's, Lyle & Kinahan
and your own York St. Flax Spinning Co. Ltd.,
where you worked with a thousand others before the war;
of trams and shopping arcades, dance-hall and 'milk bar',
cold picnics at Whitehead and Donaghadee,
of Henry Joy McCracken and Wolfe Tone,
a glimmer of hope indefinitely postponed,
daft musicals at the Curzon and the Savoy;
later, a bombing raid glimpsed from your bedroom window,
utility clothing, US armoured divisions here,
the dwindling industries. (Where now the great
liners that raised their bows at the end of the street?
Ophidian shapes among the chandeliers,
wood-boring organisms at the swirling stairs.)
Beneath a Castilian sky, at a great mystic's rococo tomb,
I thought of the plain Protestant fatalism of home.
Remember 1690; prepare to meet thy God.
I grew up among washing-lines and grey skies,
pictures of Brookeborough on the gable-ends,
revolvers, RUC, B-Specials, law-'n'-order,
a hum of drums above the summer glens
echoing like *Götterdämmerung* over lough water
in a violent post-industrial sunset blaze
while you innocently hummed 'South of the Border',
'On a Slow Boat to China', 'Beyond the Blue Horizon'.
…Little soul, the body's guest and companion,
this is a cold epitaph from your only son,
the wish genuine if the tone ambiguous.
Oh, I can love you now that you're dead and gone
to the many mansions in your mother's house.

All artifice stripped away, we give you back to nature
but something of you, perhaps the incurable ache
of art, goes with me as I travel south
past misty drumlins, shining lanes to the shore,
above the Mournes a final helicopter,
sun-showers and rainbows all the way through Louth,
cottages buried deep in ivy and rhododendron,
ranch houses, dusty palms, blue skies of the republic...

Glyn Maxwell

MY GRANDFATHER AT THE POOL

i.m. James Maxwell 1895–1980

This photo I know best of him is him
With pals of his about to take a swim,

Forming a line with four of them, so five
All told one afternoon, about to dive:

Merseysiders, grinning and wire-thin,
Still balanced, not too late to not go in,

Or feint to but then teeter on a whim.
The only one who turned away is him,

About to live the trenches and survive,
Alone, as luck would have it, of the five.

Four gazing at us levelly, one not.
Another pal decided on this shot,

Looked down into the box and said *I say*
And only James looked up and then away.

I narrow my own eyes until they blur.
In a blue sneeze of a cornfield near Flers

In 1969, he went *Near here*

It happened and he didn't say it twice.
It's summer and the pool will be like ice.

Five pals in Liverpool about to swim.
The only one who looks away is him.

The other four look steadily across
The water and the joke they share to us.

Wholly and coldly gone, they meet our eyes
Like stars the eye is told are there and tries

To see – all pity flashes back from there,
Till I too am the unnamed unaware

And things are stacked ahead of me so vast
I sun myself in shadows that they cast:

Things I dreamt but never dreamt were there,
But are and may by now be everywhere.

When you're what turns the page or looks away.
When I'm what disappears into my day.

DEEP SORRINESS ATONEMENT SONG

for missed appointment, BBC North, Manchester

The man who sold Manhattan for a halfway decent bangle,
He had talks with Adolf Hitler and could see it from his angle,
And he could have signed the Quarrymen but didn't think they'd
                                                    make it
So he bought a cake on Pudding Lane and thought 'Oh well I'll
                                                    bake it'
    But his chances they were slim,
    And his brothers they were Grimm,
    And he's sorry, very sorry,
    But I'm sorrier than him.

And the drunken plastic surgeon who said 'I know, let's enlarge 'em!'
And the bloke who told the Light Brigade 'Oh what the hell, let's
                                                    charge 'em,'
The magician with an early evening gig on the *Titanic*
And the Mayor who told the people of Atlantis not to panic,
    And the Dong about his nose,
    And the Pebble *re* his toes,
    They're all sorry very sorry,
    But I'm sorrier than those.

And don't forget the Bible, with the Sodomites and Judas,
And Onan who discovered something nothing was as rude as,
And anyone who reckoned it was City's year for Wembley,
And the kid who called Napoleon a shortarse in assembly,
    And the man who always smiles
    'Cause he knows I have his files,
    They're all sorry, really sorry,
    But I'm sorrier by miles.

And Robert Falcon Scott who lost the race to a Norwegian,
And anyone who's ever spilt the pint of a Glaswegian,
Or told a Finn a joke or spent an hour with a Swiss-German,

Or got a mermaid in the sack and found it was a merman,
    Or him who smelt a rat,
    And got curious as a cat,
    They're all sorry, deeply sorry,
    But I'm sorrier than that.

All the people who were rubbish when we needed them to do it,
Whose wires crossed, whose spirit failed, who ballsed it up or
   blew it,
All notches of *nul points* and all who have a problem Houston,
At least they weren't in Kensington when they should have been at
                                                     Euston.

For I didn't build the Wall
And I didn't cause the Fall
But I'm sorry, Lord I'm sorry,
I'm the sorriest of all.

The Best First Collection Poems

Olivia Byard

WHORES IN AMSTERDAM

I could not squeeze past their glass to join them,
even in nightmare, so I held back, shy,
while they sat or prowled, divided by reflections
from the milling crowds. Did they dream
of suburban homes before time could weave lace scars
across their thighs and find them sprawled
in cheap cubicles down dirtier alleyways,
pleading for glances from passing vagrants,
as their elder sisters did? Couldn't they reckon
the future? For now, their bodies proud,
they strutted; ultra-violet picking out in white
each frill of negligée, each curved hip:
like frothy sugar icing on birthday cake.
They seemed not to crave display:
bored as they were by the ogling men,
until one, more brave, was plucked in,
a fish from murky water, and swallowed whole
down the business end where beds gaped anatomically
and toilets waited patiently for tit-bits.
Curtains closed on this finale and we left.
Why did I come, and why return next day
en route to the Oudekerk? Why gaze
at my reflection in empty panes,
stork bundles of laundry, the carpet stains?
Was it to learn the limits of my own dark side,
what, if pressed, I could or could not, do?
Or even hide?

Theft

Her childhood was thieved, not at night
when terrors beat wings, but while the sun
reared helpless against window panes
before falling hard from the sky's arms.
Since then she has mourned in a twilight
that lurks to catch dark.

The whole thing reminds her of rings
on men's fingers: tight rings that scratch flesh,
like chalk across a blackboard.
Even the memory of her own reflection
jars with its companion glass of
dentists' drills, blood in baths.

His legs were everywhere; his touch
a careless sting; she knows
she should no longer cringe, but,
helpless, screams at smallish spiders
that crawl on grubby porcelain. An old
thief stole her youth, junked it afterward.

Sarah Corbett

WOOD SISTER

You have grown from the missed beat of my heart,
a slough of dry skin, a lost hair.

Your flesh is in my hands,
an envelope of you to be steamed and opened –

the long scar of your back, the bones of your feet,
the jut of hip holding its force.

I unfold your ears, where dirt moulds,
treasures to be snuffed out and eaten;

I can taste the dead wood of my dreams on you,
crawling from your splits and seams.

We earth here, this dark place is home.
Only the moon shows through the cracks in our skin.

The Red Wardrobe

The red wardrobe where you shut in my sister,
the iron key sliding into your pocket.

The red wardrobe that fell on my sister,
its colour old blood and rusty oil
on the soft blue insides of her elbows, her wrists,

like the Chinese burns she gave me
as I cried and hated her, until I remembered
how she made herself small in corners,
how I thought she was a kitten crying until I shook her.

The red wardrobe, its doors opening and closing in my dream,
the warm nuts in its dust becoming mice eyes,
their long tails, scratching,

that my father splintered and burnt
the day all the women left and we had fireworks.

Paul Farley

TREACLE

Funny to think you can still buy it now,
a throwback, like shoe polish or the sardine key.
When you lever the lid it opens with a sigh
and you're face-to-face with history.
By that I mean the unstable pitch black
you're careful not to spill, like mercury

that doesn't give any reflection back,
that gets between the cracks of everything
and holds together the sandstone and bricks
of our museums and art galleries;
and though those selfsame buildings stand
hosed clean now of all their gunk and soot,

feel the weight of this tin in your hand,
read its endorsement from one Abram Lyle
'Out of the strong came forth sweetness'
below the weird logo of bees in swarm
like a halo over the lion carcass.
Breathe its scent, something lost from our streets

like horseshit or coalsmoke; its base note
a building block as biblical as honey,
the last dregs of an empire's dark sump;
see how a spoonful won't let go of its past,
what the tin calls back to the mean of its lip
as you pour its contents over yourself

and smear it into every orifice.
You're history now, a captive explorer
staked out for the insects; you're tarred
and feel its caul harden. The restorer
will tap your details back out of the dark:
close-in work with a toffee hammer.

(for Julian Turner)

I found a guidebook to the port he knew
intimately – its guano-coated ledges,
its weathervanes, his bird's-eye river view
of liner funnels, coal sloops and dredgers.
It helped me gain a foothold – how he felt
a hundred rungs above a fifties street,
and whether, being so high, he ever dwelt
on suicide, or flummoxed his feet
to last night's dance steps, still fresh in his head.
It's all here in his ledger's marginalia:
how he fell up the dark stairwell to bed
and projected right through to Australia;
and said a prayer for rainfall every night
so he could skip his first hungovered round.
The dates he's noted *chamois frozen tight
into bucket*. When he left the ground
a sense of purpose overtook and let
a different set of laws come into play:
like muezzins who ascend a minaret
to call the faithful of a town to pray.
Take one step at a time. Never look down.
He'd seen the hardest cases freeze halfway,
the arse-flap of their overalls turn brown.
As a rule, he writes, *your sense of angle
becomes acute at height.* A diagram
he's thumbnailed shows a drop through a triangle
if you miscalculated by a gram.
Sometimes, his senses still blunted from booze,
he'd drop his squeegee, watch it fall to earth
and cling onto the grim hypotenuse
of his own making for all he was worth.
He seems to have enjoyed working that hour
the low sun caught the glass and raised the ante

on every aerial, flue and cooling tower,
and gilded the lofts, the rooftop shanty
town, when everything was full of itself,
and for a while even the Latin plaques
ignited with the glow of squandered wealth.
At times like these I see what our world lacks,
the light of heaven on what we've produced
and here some words lost where his biro bled
then *clouds of dark birds zero in to roost.*
There's IOUs and debtors marked in red
and some description of the things he saw
beyond the pane – a hard-lit typing pool,
a room of faces on some vanished floor
closed off and absolute like a fixed rule.
His story of the boy butting a wall,
the secretary crying at her desk,
all happened in the air above a mall.
Each edifice, each gargoyle and grotesque,
is gone. The earliest thing I remember:
as our van dropped a gear up Brownlow Hill
I looked back at the panes of distemper
that sealed a world. We reached our overspill,
and this is where our stories overlap.
The coming of the cradle and sheet glass
was squeezing out the ladder and the slap
of leather into suds, and less and less
work came through the door. And anyway
you were getting too old for scaling heights.
Now, when I change a bulb or queue to pay
at fairs, or when I'm checking in for flights,
I feel our difference bit down to the quick.
There are no guidebooks to that town you knew
and this attempt to build it, brick by brick,
descends the page. I'll hold the foot for you.

Jean Sprackland

The Ringlet

It begins like this:
a rumour tears through the class.
You search your memory and can find only
a shiny brown ringlet of hair
like an impossibly perfect shell
spread on the shoulder of another girl
and how utterly you had to touch it.
The boys laugh, the girls scuttle and whisper.
Your last friend passes you a note in Chemistry:
I can't afford to be seen with you.
You write underneath: *I wish I was dead*
and you're surprised at the truth of it.
She holds the paper to the bunsen burner
till you smell scorched fingernails.

This is how you learn it all wrong, how
you take on the lie. They start to scare you,
the motorbike girls who meet in the woods,
cropped and booted. You'll never be in their gang.
Women are not to be together
and you should not have touched the ringlet.
You watch the boys in the yard,
kicking, spitting, scuffling in the dust.
There must be something you haven't understood.

In the Planetarium

The onset of unearned night, just before
constellations dream themselves into existence.
The Plough, Orion's Belt, the Seven Sisters
plotting the emptiness above the miniature cityscape.
The moment when the lights go down,
the small dome opens out softly
into infinite dark, can make you cry. A gift

like the dive into darkness in my childhood home,
maybe once a month, when the power went off,
the TV image imploding into a small bright spot
like a dying star. There would be a lapse,
a gorgeous warm darkness you could feel on your skin

before the three of us scrambled for the pantry
to work the trip-switch. The smell of potatoes
and fruit cake. Slatted shelves you'd crack your head on
in the shove to be the bringer of light.
But here, gazing up into the vault,
I remember once, when both brothers were out,
slipping quietly in, feeling for the switch
and waiting. Listening to the dark, beyond
the buzzing of the fusebox. Wanting it to stay.

David Wheatley

LYING IN LATE

Is there a history of wasted time?
Lying in late in a sweaty T-shirt and boxer
shorts I think I'm it, not moving a whisker.
The sheets around me are tossed like the scene of a crime.

A jacket I've draped on a chair is shrugging one shoulder.
There's no saying now what use the hours I've lost track
of could have been put to, or how to fill the remainder
till night; the one urgent thing is an itch in my back.

It strikes me again that the pillow has one head too few.
My eyes shut, I daydream another. The other is you:
you last till I blink, but leave the print of your head,

I'm convinced, on the linen, and with it a strand of your hair.
A deserted house I could live with, but one deserted
by you... Old haunter, come clean: is that you not there?

BRAY HEAD

A whisper of breeze parting the pubic gorse;
the startled scald crow leaves only its shadow.
Further off a ferry scabs the sea.
The taste of the gorse heavy in the air.
The one thing the fog over the mountain
lifts on this morning disturbing the scene

is me, tracing a line over the mountain
between the plain and twitching sea,
the sound of my footsteps troubling the air
as little as my figure alters the scene.
The single crow hanging over the gorse
covers my face with its shadow

and is gone as quickly towards the sea.
Ahead a summit beacon brands the air
where one rocky outcrop commands the scene.
Walking over the brow of the mountain,
I find myself trying to keep up with my shadow
steering ahead of me between the gorse.

I feel on the point of vanishing into the air:
I want to rise like the crow in the gorse,
sheer above its earthbound shadow
and silently as the thousand-feet-below sea,
dwindle to a tinier mark on the scene
than the footprints I leave on the mountain

and vanish unnoticed from the scene.
Shadows of clouds over the mountain
creep so far along the gorse
I hardly know the mountain from the shadow,
all perched between the plain and sea
like a landscape carved out of silence in air,

mountain, mountain path, the whole in shadow,
the fog a curtain lifted on the scene:
I making my way across the mountain,
the air so nearly alive with the smell of the gorse
and the ferry dark against the air,
somewhere the mountain meets the sky and sea.

The last fog-wisp lifts above the mountain.
One scald crow alighting in the gorse
is suddenly enough to complete the scene.

The Best Individual Poems

Douglas Dunn

A European Dream

I dreamt I missed the bus from Lornza down to Warsaw.
It was raining, a rain that varnished skin and clothes.
I wandered past the turn for Ostralenka, preferring
Views of thin horses in pastures by the stagnant roadside
To thumbable cars and big trucks from Gdynia.
Policemen, farmers, and postmen with airmails passed me;
They paid me no attention, in my thornproof Border tweeds,
My briefcase and umbrella, as my Scottish brogues
Leathered the tarmac, a credit to Hoggs of Fife.
They might have thought me just another journalist
Pedestrian factfinding in industrial Ruritania
Instead of someone dreaming what almost happened.
Words in my mouth, as I talked to myself, were strangers
To each other. Crossroads' traffic, changing gear in Polish,
Was language of great charm and great Copernicus,
Spoken Chopin, the passion of Slavonic eloquence.
Night fell with cushioned landings on the active forests.
Wooded nocturnes made me feel that the continent
Widened across humanity's north-European plain
As tops of conifers twinkled in the starlight
With epic whisperings that said *"Pan Tadeusz, Pan Tadeusz"*.
Wolf, bear and bison staggered from the dens of species,
Hunted down, parked, tamed, zoo'd, or modernized,
Turned into jerkins or the privileged plateful.
Time, too, was walking in the night, counting the graves,
Re-paragraphing chronicles of howls and tears.
I heard a river wash its scraps of sunken armour.
Sword-shards, helmets, crankshafts, to a listening ear
Sounded as sub-aqueous and subterranean nudges
On skulls and bones and residue of hoof and steel,
Eyes and flesh, the pure substance of massed memories, melted
Into historical compost. I dreamt the darkest night
I ever knew and if time was strolling beside me

Down that road at the hour of no cars and no one, time
Felt disinclined to lend a hand and help me through.
"Feel hard and think historical" – I left the road
Out of obedience to my sturdy aphorism
With golf umbrella up and a firmly gripped briefcase
And through long, lighted windows I saw kissing of hands
At a big do beneath archaic chandeliers
As chauffeurs polished limousines by candlelight,
Their little vodkas balanced on their polished cars.
For several surreal moments I was at the soirée
Kissing the hand of this one, that one, being diplomatic,
Temporarily suave in black tie and dinner jacket
Or just as out-of-place in Border tweed (three-piece)
Among the ball-gowned and Old European tuxedo'd
Counts and Margraves, leaders, luminaries, a cardinal,
A consumptive poet, generals, celebrated courtesans,
Which is to say too little of East Prussians,
Muscovian footpads, Lithuanians and leather Scots
Pedlars and mercenaries, Swedes, Red Cavalrymen,
Ubiquitous Italian waiters and Parisian chefs
Voluble with genius and pedigree'd certification,
Greatcoated Tartar grooms and Cossack major-domos.
Then I was fighting off the tugs and rips of briers
In multiplying forests, or watching my wife
Led one way and my children the other, myself that way,
At the dummy station among the tight-leashed dogs
In the stench of cattle-truck excrement, with glimpsed timetables
Listing departures for Vienna, and *that* city, and *that* town,
And the grin of the officer with his hands on his hips.
Bon voyage! I shouted, as I ran through the forest
In the endless night, very deep with timber inwit,
Running like a tormented innocent through slumber
Twisted by European odiousness and what happened
In that neck of the woods. *Bon voyage!* I cried again
To myself and the millions as I ran on,
Umbrella ripped from my hand and my briefcase dropped
Into a gurgling drainage ditch, my "life's work"

Bundled down to its watery rot where croaking toads live
And my suit made by Stewart and Christie of Edinburgh
Ripped into the rags of one hungering for want, torn by
Hunger for hunger and a loud curse on all comfort,
Hunger for lyrical anger, for righteous indignation,
Vituperative and lonely in the forests of hopelessness.
I woke up as a man beaten, scratched and filthy
In the torn clothes of an interior adventure
Shouting, "Shrive me more for what I haven't committed!
Negate even my soul if I have one as I plead before
The pagan God of kindness who doesn't exist!"
History's wide-boys and murderers tittered and giggled,
Experts in *mauvaise foi*, forgetfulness, and shameless
Persistence in their arts of perpetuity and success.
"Goodbye," I said to myself, parting company with
My own certainties, my body, my name, my language.
It is disagreeable, to tend your garden, on your knees,
With the sensation of tending millions of graves.

Paul Muldoon

AFTERMATH

I

'Let us now drink,' I imagine patriot cry to patriot
after they've shot
a neighbour in his own aftermath, who hangs still between two
    sheaves
like Christ between two tousle-headed thieves,
his body wired up to the moon, as like as not.

II

To the memory of another left to rot
near some remote beauty-spot,
the skin of his right arm rolled up like a shirtsleeve,
let us now drink.

III

Only a few nights ago, it seems, they set fire to a big house and
    it got
so preternaturally hot
we knew there would be no reprieve
till the swallows' nests under the eaves
had been baked into these exquisitely glazed little pots
from which, my love, let us now drink.

Peter Porter

In the National Gallery of Victoria
Is a Nineteenth-Century genre painting
Showing a ewe on guard beside the body
Of her dead lamb while all around her sin-
black crows stand silent in the snow. Each time
I pass the picture I find I shudder twice –
Once because good taste is now endemic
And I cannot let the sentimental go
Unsneered at – I have gone to the trouble of
Acquiring words like "genre" and will call
Them to my aid – but secondly I know
I've been that ewe and soon will be that lamb;
That there's no way to love mankind but on
The improvised co-ordinates of death,
Death which rules the snow, the crows, the sheep,
The painter and the drifting connoisseur.

Enough of blood, but Abraham's raised knife
Is seldom halted and any place for God
(Even if he didn't give the orders)
Will be outside the frame. A melody
Can gong the executioner's axe awake,
A painting take away our appetite
For lunch, and mother-love still walk all night
To lull a baby quiet. Whatever gathers
Overleaf is murderous: we move
On through the gallery praising Art which keeps
The types of horror constant so that we
May go about our business and forget.

Sheenagh Pugh

Envying Owen Beattie

To have stood on the Arctic island
by the graves where Franklin's men
buried their shipmates: good enough.

To hack through the permafrost
to the coffin, its loving plaque
cut from a tin can: better.

And freeing the lid; seeing
the young sailor cocooned in ice,
asleep in his glass case.

Then melting it so gently, inch
by inch, a hundred years
and more falling away, all the distance

of death a soft hiss of steam
on the air, till at last they cupped
two feet, bare and perfect,

in their hands, and choked up,
because it was any feet
poking out of the bedclothes.

And when the calm, pinched
twenty-year-old face
came free, and he lay there,

five foot four of authentic
Victorian adventurer, tuberculous,
malnourished: John Torrington

the stoker, who came so far
in the cold, and someone whispered:
It's like he's unconscious.

Then Beattie stooped; lifted him
out of bed, the six stone
limp in his arms, and the head lolled

and rested on his shoulder,
and he felt the rush
that reckless trust sends

through parents and lovers. To have him
like that; the frail, diseased
little time-traveller;

to feel the lashes prickle
your cheek; to be that close
to the parted lips:

you would know all the fairy-tales
spoke true: how could you not try
to wake him with a kiss?

Lesley Saunders

THE USES OF GREEK

For Marjorie Rigg

'The acquisition of language is the only way of learning how to lose.'
Adam Phillips, *On Flirtation.*

i.

They went on with their meanings, oblivious –
it was part of their charm – of history's bric-à-brac;
unfazed by earthquakes in Agadir, the banging
of a shoe on a table in New York or the sudden fall
of *Poetry in Motion* from the top ten. The letters
settled in front of me like a cloud of chafers and fishmoths
crowding against a glass, just as they always had
and would: my favourites came last, χ's
elegant shears, bull-horned ψ, and φ that captained
all the words of love. In certain combinations, I learnt,
they might signify ritual murder in a palace bathroom,
a squaddie's first sight of the sea at the back end
of the mass trek through Antalya, or the kiss
a homecoming husband gobs on the shining stones
as the roaring waves paw him ashore, a near-corpse,
a slither of clammy rags over the gravel.

ii.

In the beginning we'd to master the palaver of armies –
their marches and manoeuvres, sieges and supplies,
a whisper of treachery in the mountain pass –
here were words doing duty as infantrymen, boxed
in phalanxes, safety in numbers, principal parts
on parade, commanding and being commanded.
But later, disobedient, dishevelled, they might surrender
to the inspiring breeze – leaves twittering on the holy oak,
mad semaphors. Here at last was somewhere to hide, deep

in between ἀᾶατος, inviolable and ὠώδης, egg-like, you could say
inscrutable. The boys I knew couldn't follow me there.

iii.
At the foot of the Acropolis
out in the open a man
sprang from nowhere, grabbed
my breast – at twenty I had no syntax
of demurral, no μή μ'ἐρέθιςε
of classy defiance,
only an instinctive
horrified shove, the kind
of combat you learn
in the playground,
intimate and absurd.
Mainly I felt embarrassed
as if I'd been caught peeing
in public in this sacred place.
Whatever barbarians there are
are always within. And anyway
what use is Greek to a girl?

iv.
She's turned into something that looks like old shoes or bad dreams –
once she was taller than most of the men, tattoos on her arms,
livid stipples that imprinted her with the helix-horned deer;
in her thigh boots, in her silk burial dress she rode six horses
beyond the north wind through the feather-filled air where
Herodotus wrote there were griffins guarding the gold;
but when nothing can be written, everything's in the telling
and in her tellings (we tell ourselves) she signed a way across
the trackless steppes, the endless inland archipelago set in a sea
of escaping memories. We need someone to tell our stories to,
someone to betray with each well-told tale, but who'll be the
    audience,
who the teller, who'll make sense of us, make history of us,
who'll disinter our dreams? What will we mean?

v.
Pregnant, I drove down to the holiday town one August
    afternoon
and stood on the promenade looking out to sea where he was,
in another country, ignorant. The high green swell was a
    comfort,
it answered the sea-sickness inside me. φεῦ τῆς βροτείας
φρενός[1] and I thought of all the things that make us mortal,
all the moods and voices of λύω, to loosen or undo, as in
'to loose the maiden girdle after marriage', also to set free;
or, his knees were loosened in fear, and then: she loosed
the babe from her body. Love the limb-loosener.
Λέλυνται πάντα, all is in confusion.

vi.
Parents and guardians teach us how to speak, though never quite
in words of our choosing. (Find your voice, old poets
tell the young ones, as if you could get a life by trying.)
Like the Athens orator whose father made a living selling arms
we should go on stammering, we should practise speechifying
with pebbles in our mouths. Question: were the poets lying
before they spoke? Call no-one happy until dead, is good;
but don't you think they somehow gave us too much hope?
Don't you detect a congenital elegance in those cadences,
a knee-jerk need to choose the rightest word, when really
pain's tedious and banal and getting old means life's no longer
your own, a slippage into forgetfulness, filching tomatoes, falling,
falling, not wanting to get up, the rubber sheet under you?

vii.
No redemption, then, just 'and the light's
blanked out'? Heaney gets it right –
no sin (so no forgiving), just fate
and worked-through past acts' weight –
but Harrison's déraciné too and maybe righter,
his Greek's rough-tough, a knife through butter:
'o o se toi. . . . (bracket . . . . bracket . . . .)

'o o se toi. . . . (bracket . . . . bracket . . . .)
where cows tread. . . . (track it. . . . track it. . . .)'
Fragments of a plot we can't rediscover –
a way out, or through, a way to get some cover?
A choice between the self as knower or as lover?

viii.
And mostly all there is is fragments; all
there is is mostly fragments, bright
surfaces that vibrate like splinters
of memory in the empty air, as if
in only a twinkling we were
. . . (in possession of?) . . . pity . . .
trembling . . . old age now . . .
(my) skin . . . covers . . .
(Love?) . . .
flies pursuing (the young?) . . .
glorious . . . taking (your lyre?)
sing to us of the violet-robed one
. . . especially
. . . wanders . . .[2]

ix.
This one's for muse numero nine, the last laugh,
the comic turn, the revolving door onto a naked case
of mistaken identity, the late-comer at the lit-fest,
the stand-up knock-down drop-dead art whose donkey's head
is one size fits all, invisible to the wearer, now it's your turn.
In tragedy terror's on the surface, reconciliation's profound.
Comedy tells things another way round, the joke's on us,
you're the one telling it, but it's told back to front and
you're the one telling it and you keep forgetting your lines
and time has stopped again and you're telling us we can
take a joke, oh Marjorie, what a laugh, what a hoot,
I could die laughing, did you know (of course you did)
there were once only three of them, Μελέτη, Μνήμη, Ἀοιδή,
meditation, memory, song? Two out of three ain't bad.

The opposite of memory is amnesia, also
amnesty. Who knows how much you had
to forgive and what made you translate
to Leeds from Limavaddy where they'd a high opinion
of themselves? Clouds race across the sky in gales
of laughter, gardens crack open in sly smiles,
the comedy of errors trips on, the bright surface
of things splits its sides, leaving us helpless, rocking
(in possession of?) . . . pity . . .
(Love?) . . .
. . .
. . .
sing to us . . . (?)
. . .

1   alas the mortal heart
2   lines 6-14 (section viii) are the whole of Fragment 21 in the
    Loeb *Sappho*, transl. D.A. Campbell (1990 edition).

*Marjorie Rigg, a Classical scholar, has Alzheimer's syndrome; she is my
mother in law*

The Other Poems

Peter Armstrong

NORTH OF THUNDER BAY OR HIGHWAY 61 RECONSTITUTED

What should wait for the pilgrim is sky
as wide as the Delta's but whiter,
hanging its big cold dome of a roof
over a landscape of thaws and conifers:
if you listen, the Harley's wrecked engine
will be idling down to a silence
and the wind will have picked up the phrasing
of any number of road songs,
laying its plaintive harmonica
on this consummate slow fade north.

A stride piano is echoing
further and further behind you
with its whore-house paraphernalia,
where outside on the veranda
the sun is stripping the paint down
and the street below is melting
under its white-walled tyres.
And, mornings at the edge of waking
to the droning of a Greyhound,
you have dreamed or half-remembered
the ghosts and the messiahs
in the corner of a box-car:
perfectionists of exile
with their first whiff of the frost.
From the queen bleeding in the gutter
to Zimmerman idle in Hibbing
that whole procession northbound
has rolled across the parallels
like so many great sleepers,
all bound for Sweet Home New Jerusalem,
its stock-yard square mile bellowing
and the wind on the face of the faithful

thick with Michigan's sherry wine.

But you have ridden over
a long unlyrical border,
where the ship that never came in lies
at sad perpetual anchor:
the band is playing Dixie
except the key is minor
and the roadsigns bleach to nothing
on the far side of the water.

The roadsigns bleach to nothing
and the wires sing a cappella
of a clean and rhythmless skyline
that the highway brings no nearer.
Beyond the four-shack city
with its LAST GAS BEFORE TUNDRA!
the roadsigns bleach to nothing
or they label something final:
the little, the less, and the ice-line,
the hiss at the end of the vinyl.

Kate Bingham

ETUDES

I
I woke up
with my fingers wet

but let the spills
and ridges
scab

beneath me
where I'd bled.

II
It was some weeks ago
we shared these sheets.

Sleeping alone
I've kept them so –

covered with promises
of your return,

Or reassurances
you were here –

and grown a slovenly
custodian
of love.

III
Washing my hair
you are as much perfectionist
as lover, and keep me sat there –

soap suds on my shoulders
and the bath water
going cold.

IV
My half of the bed is narrower than yours
and wrinkled with care
because the sheet will only tuck
beneath the mattress one side at a time
and this week it's your turn.

V
Let me dip my finger
in the egg-yolk of your ear;

it is eighteen days
and now my nails are long enough.

The greenhouse
harbours flies

but pollen from the tongues of lilies
is not a lovelier colour

than those flakes of wax
I yearn to print.

VI
When you are away
I sleep with cushions and books
and two hot water bottles

which I worry will burst,
leaking rubbery piss into the mattress.
I keep my underwear on

and dream of other men. Wake up
pleased to have turned them down
before it was too late.

Often the duvet will have slipped
from your side of the bed,
leaving the naked sheet smooth.

The weight of it presses me tight
against the edge. I am disorientated,
and eat cereal three times a day.

David Constantine

The Wasps

The apples on the tree are full of wasps;
Red apples, racing like hearts. The summer pushes
Her tongue into the winter's throat.

But at six today, like rain, like the first drops,
The wasps came battering softly at the black glass.
They want the light, the cold is at their backs.

That morning last year when the light had been left on
The strange room terrified the heart in me,
I could not place myself, didn't know my own

Insect scribble: then saw the whole soft
Pelt of wasps, its underbelly, the long black pane
Yellow with visitants, it seethed, the glass sounded.

I bless my life: that so much wants in.

Fred D'Aguiar

FROM BILL OF RIGHTS *(P.27)*

Someone's wife, she was Waiyaki or Makusi.
She said she washed her waist-length hair
On the stony banks of the Mazaruni.

I doubted her; not. She thought I resembled
One of C.L.R.'s Black Jacobins. I trembled
With unadulterated lust, not for her,

But for handfuls of her hair and the rest
Under us like an eiderdown in our love-nest.

Someone's wife is always sweeter
Makes you want to grab and eat her
Standing sitting lying down
Frontwards backwards round and round

Someone's wife is someone's traitor
Another's boss secretary neighbour
Standing sitting lying down
Frontwards backwards round and round

Mark Doty

GOLDEN RETRIEVALS

Fetch? Balls and sticks capture my attention
seconds at a time. Catch? I don't think so.
Bunny, tumbling leaf, a squirrel who's – oh
joy – actually scared. Sniff the wind, then

I'm off again: muck, pond, ditch, residue
of any thrillingly dead thing. And you?
Either you're sunk in the past, half our walk,
thinking of what you never can bring back,

or else you're off in some fog concerning
– tomorrow, is that what you call it? My work:
to unsnare time's warp (and woof!), retrieving,
my haze-headed friend, you. This shining bark,

a Zen master's bronzy gong, calls you here,
entirely, now: bow-wow, bow-wow, bow-wow.

Greg Delanty

THE COMPOSITOR

Perhaps it's the smell of printing ink
sets me off out of memory's jumbled font
or maybe it's the printer's lingo
as he relates how phrases came about.

How for instance: *mind your p's & q's*
has as much to do with pints & quarts
and the printer's renown for drink
as it has with those descenders.

But I don't say anything about
how I discovered where *widows & orphans*
and *out of sorts* came from the day my father
unnoticed and unexpectedly set *30*

on the bottom of his compositor's page
and left me mystified about the origins
of that end, how to measure a line gauge
and how, since he was first to go,

he slowly and without a word
turned from himself into everyone
as we turn into that last zero
before finally passing on to the stoneman.

Ian Duhig

Down in the jungle
living in a tent:
better than a prefab –
no rent!

              Children's Rhyme.

Down in the jungle going on the run,
going to get a life and going to have some fun.
Down in the jungle heading for the Smoke,
my old man's going to have a stroke.
Down in the jungle going to get a job,
going to get a flat first, no prob.

Down in the jungle, London Town,
Hope and Anchor, Cricklewood Crown,
Elephant and Castle, Rising Sun,
promises, promises, bugger all done.
Down in the jungle accommodation tied:
lost my bar job, I'm back outside.

Down in the jungle living on the street;
next to Hull this life is sweet.
Down in the jungle kipping on a bench:
beats the Riviera – no French!
Down in the jungle skippered in a squat,
better than my old man's? Do what?

Down in the jungle going on the rank,
I don't get screwed I just wank:
wank them in their Volvos, wank them in the parks,
wank them in their offices, what larks!
I'd two chances come my way:

none at all and sweet F.A.

Down in the jungle, got a proper flat,
do a bit of this and do a bit of that;
the punters come and the punters go,
suits me fine, I'm cushty cho!
Down in the jungle down on my luck?
Me downhearted? Like fuck.

Antony Dunn

Kiss

I

To explore new contours of teeth and lips,
the discovery of the tongue, like
a secret spring among rocks; this is the first
sketch of an unimaginable map.

II

Still awake as the sun stretched over the hills
to marmalade the wolds around us
we picked up our unread books
and ceased to be wheat-chameleons.
Along the greening grass we watched dawn scrubbing
night-grime from your white house, and talked
about nothing while our mouths
clamoured for toast and lip-balm.

III

Two tongues, milkshake-cool, closed in one mouth,
crushed juice from imagined strawberries.
Since that moment soft ghosts of fruit
have stalked this their dark familiar house.

IV

This kiss, the last of a multitude
which would have over-starred the universe,
is not bitter, not cold, but closed against ghosts.
Strict as the kiss of your sister's French landlady.
No Hollywood goodbye.

V

To explore new contours with an old map,
to discover only unfamiliar
fruit; this is the unimaginable
panic of homesickness. Of being lost.

Colin Falck

I dug a pond in the garden – with my lady-wife.
We shovelled great piles of concrete all one week.
You have to 'ensure the structure will not leak',
And make it look pretty too. The story of our life.

We bought some goldfish, and water-plants, and snails.
Everything flourished. That winter – '74-'75 –
The fish froze solid. (They're a kind of carp: they survive.)

We never could tell the females from the males –
Till spring. Then all demented hell broke out:
Tormented egg-fat women, with sex-crazed brutes
In hot pursuit; then – quicker than you could wish –
A pondful of fry; then a few, all darting about;
Then before we could stop it, a handful, among the roots.

– Then plants and snails, and some well-fed parent-fish.

Lavinia Greenlaw

READING AKHMATOVA IN MIDWINTER

The revelations of ice, exactly:
each leaf carries itself in glass,
each stem is a fuse in a transparent flex,

each blade, for once, truly metallic.
Trees on the hill explode like fireworks
for the minute the sun hits.

Fields hover: bleached sheets in the afternoon,
ghosts as the light goes.
The landscape shivers but holds.

Ice floes cruise the Delaware,
force it under in unnatural silence;
clarification I watch as I watch

the road – nothing but the grind of the plough
as it banks snow, drops salt and grit.
By dark these are just settled hills,

grains embedded in the new fall.
We, too, make little impression
walking back from town at midnight

on birds' feet – ducks' feet on the ramp
where we inch and scrabble our way to the door,
too numb to mind the slapstick.

How did you cross
those unlit, reinvented streets
with your fear of traffic and your broken shoe?

There are mornings when it drips and cracks.
We pull glass bars from railings,
chip at the car's shadow.

Philip Gross

12

She left home months ago.
Somehow we never noticed.
She was going solo

as a conjuror:
the egg we found rotting
in the body-folds of the sofa;

caked wads
of tissues in the bin with weetabix
compacted in them like the Mob's

car-crusher sandwiches;
potatoes spirited away
with one pass of the baggy-wristed

sweater she draped
on her bones. (What applause
when she whips it off one day

and she's gone!) Co-ordination
slipping now, caught out –
fraud, fraud! –

she plays the cheapest trick of all.
A toothmug of tap water,
sixty paracetamol.

She tries hissing herself offstage.

Sophie Hannah

Over and Elm and I

Nothing to recommend your feet
except that when you put them down
on Market Hill or Benet Street
you make a better town

Nothing to recommend your stance
except that anywhere you stand
soaks up your presence to enhance
all the surrounding land

No evidence you are a cure
but that the envelope you sealed
and hand-delivered to my door
held a St Neots field

Nothing but that you seem to reach
beyond the space you occupy
so that in March and Waterbeach
Over and Elm and Eye

pillows store imprints of your face
surprised to learn that there's a head
whose contact with a pillowcase
can so improve a bed

You hailed a taxi at the lights
now every single cab that turns
onto East Road like yours ignites
Even the downpour burns

In its stone pot the stand-up clock
turns to a flower on its stem
The county's little stations rock
I feel like one of them

David Harsent

THE CURATOR

Everything under glass and still as stone. Where an item was
out on loan, a photograph gave its likeness: at a glance,
you'd own they were little but horn and bone. 'I'm busy
just now,' he said, 'why not go on alone? You can't get
easily lost. Those arrows will bring you home.'

> *This is the razor that turned on its owner,*
> *this is the finger that fired the first shot,*
> *this is the flower that poisoned its wearer,*
> *this is the riddle that started the rot.*

But when I turned the corner, he was there; of course he was.
'Aren't we a pair?' he laughed, as if climbing the stair in step,
as if breathing that mouldy air, might make us sudden
partners in Truth-or-Dare. He thumbed the catalogue; the
sheer size of it made me stare: the weight of loss. 'Is it
something particular?' As if he didn't know. 'Is it something
awry or unfair?'

> *This is the poodle that bit Aristotle,*
> *this is the tongue with the strawberry wart,*
> *this is the rattle they found in the shtetl,*
> *this is the cutie who wouldn't abort.*

He stood at the door to see me off, and wore the cloths of
frailty like the Godless poor: which fooled me not one bit.
'You've seen damn-all, you know, but if you're sure – 'He
snicked the ID off my coat and tore the lapel a token inch. 'A
souvenir...' Now I no longer wore my face and name. 'It's
queer,' he shook my hand, 'this way or that, they all come
back for more.'

This is the tumour that grew like a rumour,
this is the rafter and this is the rope,
this is the drama that buried the dreamer,
this is the hope beyond hope beyond hope.

Geoff Hattersley

'On the Buses' with Dostoyevsky

Because of the steelworks
that deafened my dad
our telly was always
too loud, so loud
it formed a second narrative
to what I was reading
up in my room
in my late teens – I'd have
Hemingway and *Kojak*,
Alias Smith and Jones and Poe.
All that noise! Car chases
and gunshots, sirens, screams,
horse racing and boxing,
adverts for fishfingers,
floor cleaner and fresh breath;
and Knut Hamsun starving,
Ahab chasing his whale.
I felt like a learner driver
stalled at a traffic light,
a line of lorries behind me.
Because of the steelworks
that closed in 1970
and which I never saw
except as a skeleton,
I like silence and calm,
I like silence and smoke
cigarettes in the dark.

Peter Joliffe

LACUNA

sometimes still I turn to the phone
thinking I'll disturb you room to room
only to seize before I'm there
to remember that you've gone

the words I wake will not strike home
but only stray into starless air

absurd I'll not reach you again
and that there's no one now to miss

those that remain remain
in other countries
in their own time, with their own rain

Thomas Lynch

The Riddance

In her memory of it
he had never harmed her.
For weeks after the burial
he'd been so sweet.
Slow and deliberate,
he had only touched her
for pleasure, her pleasure.
Attentive to detail,
tender as newlyweds
on a kind of honeymoon,
they conducted their
intimate business in
the breathless lexicons
of hope and forgiveness.
It was only after
the casseroles had been
returned, the borrowed chairs,
the children gone home
to their other lives,
the sister moved back to the
Midwest and the thank you's
mailed out for all condolences,
that she sat in the chill parlour
of her new widowhood
remembering the bruises,
the boozy gropings,
and sad truths. And hugging herself
in the quiet she reckoned
the riddance she held there
was a good one.

Jack Mapanje

SKIPPING WITHOUT ROPE

I will, I will skip without your rope
Since you say I should not, I cannot
Borrow your son's skipping rope to
Exercise my limbs; I will skip without

Your rope as you say even the lace
I want will hang my neck until I die.
I will create my own rope, my own
Hope and skip without your rope as

You insist I do not require to stretch
My limbs fixed by these fevers of your
Reeking sweat and your prison walls;
I will, will skip with my forged hope;

Watch; watch me skip without your
Rope; watch me skip with my hope:
A-one, a-two, a-three, a-four, a-five
I will, a-seven, I do, will skip, a-ten,

Eleven, I will skip without, will skip
Within and skip I do without your
Rope but with my hope; and I will,
Will always skip you dull, will skip

Your silly rules, skip your filthy walls
Your weevil pigeon peas, skip your
Scorpions, skip your Excellency Life
Glory, I will, will skip your lot without

Breaking my neck, a-thirty, I do, I will,
Will hang your hope, I will skip my rope
Around your neck, thirty seven, thirty
Nine, I do, you don't, I can, you can't,

I will, you won't, I see, you don't, I
Sweat, you don't; I can, can wipe my
Gluey brow then wipe you at a stroke;
I will, will wipe your horrid, stinking,

Vulgar prison rules, will wipe you all
Then hop about, hop about my cell, my
Home, the mountains, my globe as your
Sparrow hops about your prison yard

Without your hope, without your rope;
I swear, I will skip without your rope, I
Declare, I will have you take me to your
Showers to bathe me where I can resist

This singing child you want to shape me
I'll fight your rope, your rules, your hope
As your gallant sparrow under your super-
vision! Guards! Take us for the shower!

Conor O'Callaghan

THE SWIMMING POOL

It goes under, the cursor, whenever I place my finger
on the space bar and hold it like this for a minute.
The blue screen shimmers the way a pool's sunlit
floor moves after the splash of a lone swimmer.

As long as this minute lasts, the season is somewhere
between July and dawn: the soundless underwater
of sandals left out overnight and garden furniture,
that will end, but could just as easily go on forever.

I could be forgiven for forgetting that it was ever there.
The pool is only still again when I take away my finger.
Unthinking, and unable to hold its breath any longer,
as much as two pages further, it comes up for air.

Marita Over

THE DAFFODILS

And now I don't know
if they were real
or in a book.

They had the look
of colluding schoolgirls,
sucking on straws,

clear-eyed, insouciant.
Launching themselves
from their vase on the sill,

or maybe a vale,
or the brow of a hill,
they were almost evangelical,

anyway, all yellow,
with a feverish faith
in something.

And I went quietly once
with a pair of silver scissors at their
bonnety optimism

to snip out their anthers
which fell
like Midas' eyelashes.

Ruth Padel

We're talking different kinds of vulnerability here.
　　These icicles aren't going to last for ever
Suspended in the ultraviolet rays of a Dumfries sun.
　　But here they hang, a frozen whirligig of lightning,
And the famous American sculptor
　　Who scrambles the world with his tripod
For strangeness au naturel, got sunset to fill them.
　　It's not comfortable, a double helix of opalescent fire

Wrapping round you, swishing your bark
　　Down cotton you can't see,
On which a sculptor planned his icicles,
　　Working all day for that Mesopotamian magic
Of last light before the dark
　　In a suspended helter-skelter, lit
By almost horizontal rays:
　　Making a mist-carousel from the House of Diamond,

A spiral of Pepsodent darkening to the shadowfrost
　　Of cedars at the Great Gate of Kiev.
Why it makes me think of opening the door to you
　　I can't imagine. No one could be less
Of an icicle. But there it is –
　　Having put me down in felt-tip
In the mystical appointment book,
　　You shoot that quick

Inquiry-glance, head tilted, when I open up,
　　Like coming in's another country,
A country you want but have to get used to, hot
　　From your *bal masqué*, making sure
That you found before's
　　Still here: a spiral of touch and go,

Lightning licking a tree
    Imagining itself Aretha Franklin

Singing you make me feel like a natural woman
    In *basso profondo,*
Firing the bark with its otherworld ice
    The way you fire, lifting me
Off my own floor, legs furled
    Round your trunk as that tree goes up
At an angle inside the lightning, roots in
    The orange and silver of Dumfries.

Now I'm the lightning now you, you are,
    As you pour yourself round me
Entirely, No who's doing what and to who,
    Just a tangle of spiral and tree.
You might wonder about sculptors who come all this way
    To make a mad thing that won't last.
You know how it is: you spend a day, a whole life.
    Then the light's gone, you walk away

To the Galloway Paradise Hotel. Pine-logs,
    Cutlery, champagne – OK,
But the important thing was making it.
    Hours, and you don't know how it'll be.
Then something like light
    Arrives last moment, at speed reckoned
Only by horizons: completing, surprising
    With its three hundred thousand

Kilometres per second.
    Still, even lightning has its moments of panic.
You don't get icicles catching the midwinter sun
    In a perfect double helix in Dumfriesshire every day.
And can they be good for each other,
    Lightning and tree? It'd make anyone,
Wouldn't it, afraid? That rowan would adore

To sleep and wake up in your arms

But's scared of getting burnt.
    And the lightning might ask, touching wood,
'What do you want of me, now we're in the same
    Atomic chain?' What can the tree say?
'Being the centre of all that you are to yourself –
    That'd be OK. Being my own body's fine
But it needs yours to stay that way.'
    No one could live for ever in

A suspended gleam-on-the-edge,
    As if sky might tear any minute.
Or not for ever for long. Those icicles
    Won't be surprise any more.
The little snapped threads
    Blew away. Glamour left that hill in Dumfries.
The sculptor went off with his black equipment.
    Adzes, twine, leather gloves.

What's left is a photo
    Of a completely solitary sight
In a book anyone can open.
    And whether our touch at the door gets forgotten
Or turned into other sights, light, form,
    I hope you'll be truthful
To me. At least as truthful as lightning,
    Skinning a tree.

Joan Jobe Smith

The Pow Wow Café

To buy herself a new 50s' moderne sofa
and wrought iron-framed repro of Picasso's
'Don Quixote' my father was too much
of a tightwad to buy her, my mother
got a job at the Pow Wow Café, a
truckstop on Highway 19 in Downey,
California where the waitresses wore
short, short red polka-dot skirts and
low-cut white peasant blouses that showed
half of my mother's baba au rhum breasts.
'No!' bellowed my father while my mother
ironed her starched uniform into stiff
Mt. Everest peaks, not speaking to him
for trying to tell her what to do.
'No!' he bellowed as she drove away
to work her first night at the Pow Wow Café
and my father put up with this for
four nights, chainsmoking, biting his
fingernails, watching tv and come Friday night
he took my mother's short, short skirt
and low-cut peasant blouse and me to the
Pow Wow Café where he threw open the
manager's office door and threw my mother's
uniform onto the floor and bellowed,
'My wife's not working in this
whorehouse any more!' and then my father
sat down at the counter with all the truckers
ordered a chocolate sundae for me, coffee,
double cream, for himself, and told the
waitress when she brought them how nice
she looked this evening.

Martin Stannard

Seeing Happy

I sent a little letter to the retired admiral
about butterflies, and their inexplicable absence
from modern theories of elegance. Goodness
knows why I had become so moany, my pen
somehow "overtaken" by a curmudgeon.
There'd been mention of a spirit who lived in the walls,
whose presence was like eggs on the underside
of nettles, a small patch of wildness in
an otherwise hopelessly tended plot of world.

Looking out of my window and seeing happy
I immediately wrote down sad, and the hours
spent pleading with the Muses that they leave off
preening their feathers a while and take a look around –
when you totted them up, they would have come to
one or two decent jobs if those little cards
in the Job centre are anything to go by.

There's nothing I don't know about futile gestures,
like, I would take the canoe out on to the lake
and challenge the sky to cloud heavily up, come on
down, and slug it out, and not notice the dragonflies
being rather marvellous over there above the reeds
or the chaffinches perched aloft airing their one note,
and forget how we would try and count their colours
until they flew off toward the highway and the smoke.

And there would be little notes pinned up around
the house in my handwriting so nobody'd miss
them, but I couldn't swear to having written them
awake. Their tone was undeniably somewhat sour,
so if you read them aloud near a jug of milk
it would go off at once, and it's beyond me to explain

why the world in its weariness would capture me
like this, engulf me in this petty fog,
when I know we're at the beginning of a new age
and there's nothing to be frightened of or blue about.

Paul Summers

i. the last bus

ONE more tedious chorus
of *suck my cocks*
& i'll be back –
back to the bookends,
the balding pebble-dash
of once-home,
to mam asleep,
& dad squinting at the match

ii. pompeii

the door will be open.
familiar stairs will greet me;
still a slither of carpeted pyramid,
still the summit of everest,
still a mystery despite all
my subsequent reasoning.
beyond, my pompeii:
a museum of bunk-beds
& scrap-books neatly housed
on formica shelves,
a squadron of airfix planes
so heavy with dust
that they are grounded.

iii. silent movie

there will be
no spoken welcomes;
perhaps a patted shoulder,
a general enquiry of mutual well-being,

an offer of alcohol or tea,
but mainly the silence
of expressionless love.
tomorrow he will bury his father.

iv. breakfast

undeterred by the seriousness
of it all, i tease mam about the
instant coffee; i have spent my
lifetime teasing their sensibilities,
made it my duty to talk politics
at every shared meal, bored them
to tears with history's injustice
& the rhetoric of struggle: not once
have i sat here just to eat. always
canvassing for approval, always
the missionary, so rarely the son.

v. eulogy

for three months they had sat like sentries
at the foot of his bed, watched him shrink,
made sense of jumbled words, poured
hundreds of glasses of lucozade,
smiled at him effortlessly when his eyes
opened briefly & at each other when they
closed again. they never missed a day.

vi. taboo

her words were like a sad old song,
each pathetic line choking her.
she spoke about dad, & how
at granda's passing he had uttered
those words: three times he'd said
i love you, his hands climbing his

father's chest like a child wanting
to be carried. it had been an hour
or more before he could see to drive.

vii. history

he had known nothing but outside toilets,
grown accustomed to draughts; thinking
our place posh with its upstairs lav. a relic
of before. he had known the harshness
of strikes, & of begging to the guardians
for a vestige of their charity. he had seen
men crushed like ripe fruit by falls of rock,
been blinded by shift-end light for almost
fifty years, & all this time a dream recurred,
a patchwork of cowboys borrowed from
libraries, of heroes with his face. he had
done without beer for weeks to buy dad's
first bike & was rarely impressed by hardship.
he was generous with his smiles, but never
to my knowledge ever once kissed my grandma:
his spine was bent, his lungs full, each scar he had,
a blue tattoo, & since his retirement he bathed
once a week & shopped nowhere but the co-op
despite mam's constant nagging.

viii. witness

witness the scarce embrace
of brothers; in doing well,
grown separate. witness
the puzzled heirs to a half built
jerusalem, guilty only of potential.
witness the prophecy of a single
hybrid rose, slave to memory,
without perfume or thorns.
witness the past, respectfully

collected at twelve careful paces;
in their parochial eyes, our ring
of blood an ivy league huddle.

ix. prodigals

we are prodigals
too long away
the orphans of nostalgia
all our singular pasts
unspendable currency
we are stranded
& this hearse
the last bus

Matthew Sweeney

Goodbye to the Sky

i.m. Michelle

Let me tell you a story you'd have liked –
a small plane gets in trouble,
has to come down on a Devon road
and when it bumps to a halt
one wing is over a hedge, the other
sticks skewways into the path of cars,
and the young pilot walks away.
But he wouldn't have known he would,
when the instruments were saying
goodbye to the sky. I hear him
shouting to his wife, his children,
praying for the first time in years,
cursing, even, calling the plane
all kinds of jerry-built junk,
wishing he hadn't been bought
Airfix planes and Biggles books,
remembering his first tonguey kiss
and the last, that morning,
his lovely wife half-asleep
but turning to him, as if continuing
a dream he was happy to share,
unlike this daylit nightmare,
the terrible ground coming closer,
the road a parody of a runway
sandwiched between hedges,
and finally the jolt of the landing,
the best and the worst he'll ever do.
He walked away, that young man,
but you didn't, and your falling
lasted years. Hear this, though –
sticking into that same Devon sky

is a black obelisk, built to remember
the Waterloo dead, its inscription
Peace to the souls of the heroes
and hear it updated, in the singular.

Chris Wallace-Crabbe

Years On

At the trailing edge of autumn
grey rain is falling hard
to soften the native grasses
in the old graveyard.

My son is tucked well under there
among the clay and stones,
though what his name betokens
is nothing more than bones.

And how long would it take for
the water to soak down
and cover every bone with
its fine, transparent gown?

I do not know, merely recall
moments of pleasure and mirth.
As he trod lightly on you,
rest lightly on him, earth.

Andrew Wilson

VODAFONE

I trusted the salesmen to be honest,
told one in each shop about us, just enough –
about the distance we lived apart, your car:
how we needed something basic, robust
that it didn't need to reach the Shetlands, round the world –
the technology of yachts, downed aeroplanes –
just between our two, well connected northern cities;
that if the batteries ran down, or it was always on the blink
you'd put it in the kitchen drawer, forget it.

But I didn't tell them how you lived alone
about the stone walls, elderly, unsure neighbours,
the overgrown hedge that might catch a shout;
or the weekends you spent sanding, painting
making everything just so;
and my one day fitting window locks
turning up jangling a bagful from Do It All:
the one too small for a cat, that I nailed shut.

And I didn't say I promise not to ring on it
you going red at its trilling in a meeting, a shop
so long as you promise to keep it by the bed –
some bits of change on my table, a used lipsyl
and on the passenger seat like a kitten in the car,
jump leads uncoiled on the floor;
but I checked the warranty, that they had branches near you,
paid for three years rental on my credit card
and went to get some book, trinket, your proper present.